MW00325856

Grinding my ink

Grinding my ink

Haiku
by Margaret Chula

Margaret Chula

Sumi Drawings
by Rhony Alhalel

Katsura Press
1993

ISBN: 0-9638551-9-0
Library of Congress No. 93-080026

Printed on recycled, acid-free paper

Katsura Press
P. O. Box 275
Lake Oswego, OR 97034

*This collection of haiku is dedicated
to the house at Icho da cho 10-1
and to John who shared it with me*

INTRODUCTION

Nearly all my memories of Japan center around a ramshackle wooden house on the northern edge of Kyoto. Most modern Japanese would have considered it uninhabitable, but for John and me it was a sanctuary, a place of quiet harmony and welcome solitude.

If one believes in geomancy, the house was ideally situated at the edge of a hillside which was engraved with the Chinese characters *Myo* and *Ho* (marvelous law of the Buddha). Every summer the villagers of Matsugasaki light these configurations with bonfires to guide the spirits of their ancestors, who come down for the festival of Obon. On New Year's Eve we would join our neighbors in ringing the huge brass bell at Yusen-ji, the oldest Nichiren sect temple (built in the fourteenth century). Mt. Hiei was visible from our kitchen window, and just outside the back door lay rice paddies and fields of vegetables that changed with the seasons. 'Lady Bountiful,' our favorite farmlady, peddled her produce from a cart which she pulled through the neighborhood, exchanging gossip along the way.

Our dirt lane of ten traditional houses was indeed a microcosm in a rapidly encroaching city. It became known as 'Gaijin Mura' (foreigners' village) because all but two of the houses were occupied by Westerners. Due to strict government regulations, the elderly Japanese couples who also lived there had been paying the same rent for thirty years. The landlady therefore preferred foreigners–most did not stay long and new tenants could be charged more. John and I, however, stayed for twelve years and were the last occupants of Gaijin Mura.

When we moved into Icho da cho 10-1 in the fall of 1980, it had been vacant for about two years except for spiders, bees and mice. The bees and mice soon found other lodgings; the giant black spiders remained but restricted themselves to a corner of the in-house outhouse. Encouraged by the fact that there were no broken windows, we set about making the house livable. We scrubbed away fifteen layers of torn paper and stretched new paper onto the opaque *fusuma* room divider doors, replaced the *washi* on the eight *shoji*, plugged up leaks in the cedar tub, and even ventured to replaster the walls by layering a sandy mixture onto them with a trowel. Unlike the Japanese, we didn't worry about not being professionals at these tasks–we just did them and were satisfied with the results. Traditional houses, especially those built just after the war when quality materials were scarce, are of a fragility that most Americans cannot imagine.

The house and garden were in constant need of maintenance. John would periodically climb up on the roof to push tiles back into place, particularly during the rainy season. Every spring and autumn we pruned pine trees and camellias and maples to allow sunlight into the house. Weeding the moss garden became a daily meditation. The toilet (a separate room from the bath) was dimly lit and made aesthetically pleasing with a Kabuki calendar and *ikebana*. Every six weeks, a truck would come to pump out the pit. In the interim, we relied on a primitive electric fan attached to the exhaust stack outside the house to draw out the odor. One sultry day it became obvious that the fan was not doing its job. We discovered that the neighbor's wisteria vine had twined up to our roof, wound itself around the rotating fan, and strangled it!

In a Japanese house there is a very thin line between the outdoors and indoors–breached by many cracks and crevices. Animals felt free to enter and settle in. Every winter we heard the sounds of mice nesting in the closet, and for a few weeks a weasel made his nightly visit to the garbage can in the back hallway until John secured the lid with a sailor's knot. On summer evenings, baby *tanuki* (raccoon dogs) frolicked in the garden and fearlessly tried to leap up onto the *tatami* through the open *shoji*. During the rainy season, six-inch centipedes scuttled across the damp walls and moths did their frantic dance inside paper lanterns. On our last day, a cold bleak February afternoon, just after the moving company had taken away the final crate, a red fox flashed by the window.

Icho da cho is now a deserted lane of houses in various stages of collapse. It is only a matter of time before they are torn down and the valuable land converted into parking lots or white-tiled apartment buildings. All the trees will be destroyed, the gardens paved over and the stepping stones crushed into gravel. The old Japanese couples have died and the foreigners have moved on. There remain only the black spiders who weave their memories into a hundred fragile webs.

Portland, Oregon
February 1993

about the title

The bamboo brush waits patiently next to the sheet of *washi* as a small amount of water is poured onto the *suzuri* (inkstone). Picking up the ink stick, the artist begins to rub the *sumi* back and forth in the slow process of making ink. Back and forth it scrapes against the unyielding stone, screeching like the monkey mind within. The artist continues grinding the ink stick until the water begins to dissolve its edges, until all sound is dampened, until all that remains is the steady motion.

As the color deepens and ink fills the hollow of the *suzuri*, the artist's mind begins to empty. All thoughts of past and future are left behind in this repetitive motion of the present and one enters the state of 'no mind' or '*muga*,'

the silence between the notes of a flute
the white space around an ink drawing
that which is left unsaid.

Flower *(Hana)*

grinding my ink—
a black cat
howls in childbirth

boys' running team
the crackle
of polyester

threading its song
into the wind
mountain cuckoo

a field of buttercups
white moths
changing color

smell of narcissus
   my thirteenth spring
   and Mother's tumor

warbler's song
welcomes me home
   the prowling cat

making it harder
to trim the tree
a perfect web

plowing the paddy
myna birds marching
                just behind

cow dung, chicken dung
dug into the new garden
the cat adds his own

in strawmat raincoats
farmers plant rice
their boots croaking

jogging past
a pond of purple iris
twilight thickens

wisteria
   its reflection
buzzing

spring cleaning
   a white kitten
rolls in the dust

orange tulips
        swallow
the sunset

past the hunchback
    father races
        with his sons

airing the futon
on the first day of sunshine
  bulbul fluffs his wings

Sento Palace
burnt again and again
 flaming azaleas

          last blossoms
man in a wheelchair
wheels by slowly

saying good-bye
tinkling
　　of a wind chime

morning twilight

(Ayabe, Japan)

morning twilight
beyond the raindrops
the first bird song

walking into silence
startled
by a flutter of wings

he keeps turning around—
the black cat I follow
into the fog

soft spring rain
the cat licks
the cabbage leaves

rutted path
strewn with sasanquas
my first corsage

floating in the pond
where the old woman drowned
red camellia heads

returning
the borrowed umbrella
splattered with blossoms

Fire *(Hi)*

sawing afternoon
into evening
cicadas

Hiroshima heat
mother and daughter
fold a thousand cranes

teacher's question
hangs in the drowsy classroom
a crow answers

all at once
peony blossoms drop
clap of thunder

morning yoga
　　a frog in the garden
mimics my pose

slide open the *shoji*
to the heat of the garden
faded cockscomb

resting in the shade
farmwomen gossip
ripe tomatoes

typhoon rains
    a summer monarch
hangs upside down

stars, stars' reflections
mirrored in the paddy field
oh! the fireflies

cosmos tossing
in the noonday sun
first love

sound of a moth
trapped in a paper lantern
summer rain

they have discovered
my flowered kimono
those relentless ants

twilight
    the weeds escape
    grandfather's eyes

cicadas—
the tree root
pulses

late afternoon
   carp whiskers
   reflect the sun

cave in the forest
where a monk chanted sutras
   hum of mosquitoes

blue butterfly
on a slate-gray tile
sound of a stream

at the Noh play

at the Noh play
a woman follows her text
   dirt under her nails

       old man speaks
       the breath
          before the sound

white *tabi*
circle the stage
   walk a hundred miles

old Noh actor
hands soft as a girl's
    the quivering fan

      front row seat
      sparkles of sweat
      on the back of his hand

      closing his fan
      the cool fragrance
      of a kimono sleeve

shakuhachi
stillness of water
in a stone basin

Moon   *(Tsuki)*

outside the empty hut
a huddle of crickets
their hollow voices

morning glories
fold into seedpods
   yet another autumn

on the train
the smell of mothballs
early chill

cold wind stirs my hair
and the fern fronds
    the bald Buddha

at the mountain shrine
a nun claps her hands
caw! caw!

wind blows
    the last brown leaves
clenched fingers

stalking the heron
old man in a black beret
aims his zoom lens

pomegranates
burst open on the ground
  sputtering sparrows

hanging the rice at dusk
the weary farmer
still wears his straw hat

dragonflies thrum
over the rice stubble
earthenware sunset

brown-robed monk
raking leaves into neat piles
his new Adidas

old woman
and lotus leaves
bow low to the pond

typhoon wind
rips tiles from our roof
the web intact

sudden shower
in the empty park
   a swing still swinging

flying through gingkos
and then the maples
how black the crow!

under the full moon
plumes of pampas
   the cat's tail twitches

plump persimmon
plops into the pond
smell of mud

watching the fish pond
fill up with shadows
a distant train

in autumn
nesting birds   part
in mid air

my even breath
joins the misty night
  steam from the teabowl

lying side by side
separate letters
from our divorced friends

sweeping, sweeping, sweep—
the old woman's broom
no match for the wind

decayed leaves
the pond
their color

graveyard poet

(Hotaka, Japan Alps)

birds of prey
gather
in leafless trees

on the gravestone
a mouse nibbles the apple
hawk circles

scaring the hawks
away from their midday meal
graveyard poet

how hard the gravestone
an ant disappears
into the crevice

floating in the *sake*
left for the beloved
a moth

summer lanterns
hang from the new tombstone
crumbling chrysanthemums

dead people
dead flowers
clouds pass

write me a haiku
in two languages
for my gravestone

Snow *(Yuki)*

walking north
the wind blows
my breath behind me

tree limb shadows
blow across the *shoji*
mice in the closet

hearing the whack
of the Zen master's stick
my own shoulders twitch

the sun sets
behind winter trees
last persimmon

hibachi embers—
red berries
dusted with snow

sunlight on *tatami*
the old Buddhist temple
smells of chrysanthemums

long winter night
tangerine peels
piling up

even the crow's call
is muffled in the snowfall
this cold, cold morning

bare tree limbs
the candle flickers
in the stone garden

rotenburo
cedars sprinkled with snow
and sulphur steam

icicles form
    and melt
housebound

winter afternoon
grebe swims into the shadows
  its wake trilling

heavy with snow
  the branch
  its shadow

at year's end
I burn the Daruma doll
with only one eye

hanging New Year's cards
on the *shoji*
    last year's dust

pounding rice cakes
the sky turns
from blue to gold

no footprints
outside the hermit's hut
on New Year's day

wrapping my hands
round the warm teacup
the waning moon

silence
white camellias
in a chipped vase

dead sparrow

(for Matsumura-san)

our cheerful neighbor
brings us eggs and *soba*
before she dies

how could I know
it was the last time
her shuffling feet

curled up on *tatami*
with legs loosely bound
dead sparrow*

* Japanese women bind their legs together for modesty
before committing suicide.

on the second floor
corpse
with the night light on

in the silence
snipping off the flowers' heads
click of scissors*

into the coffin
I place the white chrysanthemum
over her slashed wrist

paying respects
wiping my nose on the rough wool
of my black coat

* A funeral attendant cuts off the blossoms and offers
them to the mourners on a tray.

from the house altar
her photograph smiles down
on her waxen face

blue-tinted corpse
bound in funeral sheets
fresh pine boughs

not looking at
the new stitches above her eye
her laughter

saying good-bye
snow melting
from the roof tiles

fat woman weeps
as the hearse drives away
then powders her face

at my doorstep
adding the salt
to the new snow*

after her funeral
a spring *ikebana*
in the *tokonoma*

* For purification

GLOSSARY

bulbul—a common gray bird, about the size of a jay

Daruma doll—*papier mâché* figurine on which you draw one eye as you make a wish or set a goal, adding the other when it is fulfilled

hibachi—large ceramic urn containing charcoal, often placed in temples for guests to warm their hands over as they view the garden

ikebana—flower arrangement

Noh—stylized Japanese theater evolved in the fourteenth century for aristocrats. Actors perform in elaborate costumes accompanied by a chorus and musicians. The archaic language cannot be comprehended by modern-day Japanese, who must bring their own scripts to follow the story.

rotenburo—open-air bath

sasanqua—a kind of camellia

shakuhachi—bamboo flute with a haunting tone

shoji—a sliding wooden door comprised of an open lattice covered with a single layer of translucent paper

soba—buckwheat noodles, eaten especially at New Year's for long life

sutra—Sanskrit term for Buddhist scripture

tabi—formal pure white socks, divided like a mitten; the only footwear of the Noh actor

tatami—woven matted floors found in traditional Japanese homes and in temples

tokonoma—an alcove in the main room where a scroll and flower arrangement are displayed

Some of these haiku have been previously published in the following periodicals and anthologies:

Modern Haiku
Virtual Image
Dragonfly
Frogpond
Cicada
Brussel Sprout
GEPPO
Mainichi Daily News
Kansai Time Out
Kyoto Journal
Kaleidoscope
Poetry Nippon
KO
Winter's Blossom (New Zealand)
The Rise and Fall of Sparrows
*Haiku Moment: An Anthology of
    North American Haiku*

Margaret Chula lived in Kyoto, Japan, for twelve years where she taught creative writing and haiku at Doshisha Women's College and Kyoto Seika University. Her haiku have received awards from *Modern Haiku, Brussel Sprout, Mainichi Shimbun,* and Gifu Women's University. In 1987 she placed second in the Japan Airlines/*Mainichi Daily News* National Haiku Contest. Itoen Tea Company selected one of her haiku for a publicity poster which was displayed in train stations throughout Japan. In 1993 she won the Japan Tanka Poets Club Prize in the Third International English Tanka Contest. Her haiku have been included in the prestigious *Anthology of North American Haiku Writers* and collected in the Museum of Haiku Literature in Tokyo. In 1982 her short story 'The Comb' placed first in the Tokyo English Literature Society's short story contest and was broadcast over BBC's World Service the following year. While in Kyoto, she also studied *hanga* (woodblock printing) and *ikebana*, receiving a teacher's license from the Sogetsu School. She is currently living in a 100-year-old house in Portland, Oregon.

Rhony Alhalel is a painter, calligrapher and graphic designer. Born in Peru, he now lives between Reykjavik, Kyoto, New York and Lima. He has had several one-man shows in each of these cities and is the graphic designer for *Kyoto Journal.*

Design and layout by John A. Hall
Katsura Press logo created by Suellen Larkin
Set in Adobe Garamond
Printed on Champion Pageantry Smooth Porcelain stock
by Ash Creek Press, Portland, OR
Perfect bound at Specialty Bindery, Washougal, WA